The Student's
TOOLBOX

TIPS FOR BETTER LISTENING

ROBYN HARDYMAN

Gareth Stevens
Publishing

Please visit our website, www.garethstevens.com. For a free color catalog of all our high-quality books, call toll free 1-800-542-2595 or fax 1-877-542-2596.

Library of Congress Cataloging-in-Publication Data

Hardyman, Robyn.
Tips for better listening / Robyn Hardyman.
    pages cm. -- (The student's toolbox)
Includes bibliographical references and index.
ISBN 978-1-4824-0175-2 (pbk.)
ISBN 978-1-4824-0176-9 (6-pack)
ISBN 978-1-4824-0174-5 (library binding)
1. Listening. 2. Students--Life skills guides. I. Title.
BF323.L5H36 2014
371.30281--dc23

2013028353

First Edition

Published in 2014 by
Gareth Stevens Publishing
111 East 14th Street, Suite 349
New York, NY 10003

© 2014 Gareth Stevens Publishing

Produced by Calcium, www.calciumcreative.co.uk
Designed by Emma Debanks and Paul Myerscough
Edited by Sarah Eason and Ronne Randall

Photo credits: Cover: Shutterstock: Monkey Business Images. Inside: Shutterstock: Matthew Benoit 29, Bikeriderlondon 6, George Dolgikh 7, Jaimie Duplass 14, Szasz-Fabian Ilka Erika 26, Olesya Feketa 9, 16, 22, Goodluz 20, 21, Oleksiy Mark 25, Felix Mizioznikov 12, Monkey Business Images 1, 11, 17, 23, 27, 28, Natursports 4, Pressmaster 15, Prudkov 18, Alexander Raths 19, Richard Thornton 5, YanLev 10, 24, Lisa F. Young 8, ZouZou 13.

Printed in the United States of America

CPSIA compliance information: Batch #CW14GS: For further information contact Gareth Stevens, New York, New York at 1-800-542-2595.

CONTENTS

WHY SHOULD WE LISTEN?

Have you ever been in a noisy playground, where everyone is shouting at once and the traffic is rushing by on the street? You hear all these sounds, but what are you listening to? Are you listening to your friend? Perhaps you are listening to the teacher calling you inside? Listening is not the same as hearing. Listening is a very important part of a student's toolbox. It's fun, too!

Good listening is at the heart of learning.

Active Listening

Hearing is a passive activity. This means that we hear without trying to—our ears receive sounds whether we like it or not. Listening is active—we choose what we listen to and what we pay attention to. Listening is one of the most important tools for learning. It is also an important tool for life in general. Good listening is at the heart of all our understanding, and our communication with other people. Students who listen well perform better than those who do not.

Everyone needs to be able to listen to instructions.

WHY LISTEN?

Active listeners listen closely and carefully to gain knowledge and understanding. Here are some of the reasons why you should listen actively:

- **Listening in class:** Much of what you are taught is explained verbally by your teachers. You must be able to pay attention and to think about what you hear.

- **Responding well:** Try to listen to the ideas and opinions of others. If you listen well, you will be able to respond and hold useful discussions with the speaker.

- **Developing concentration and memory:** Good listening develops your concentration and memory skills.

- **Attracting people:** If you are a good listener, others will be drawn to you. If people think you understand them, they will want to talk to you.

- **Staying safe:** It can be dangerous not to listen. Instructions and warnings are often spoken to us.

CHAPTER TWO

ENGAGING WITH THE SPEAKER

There are some simple tips that will help you with all kinds of listening in school. Following these basic rules helps when you engage with another person. When you are listening to the teacher reading an informational text aloud or speaking to you about a topic, or when you are listening to a discussion between other pupils, follow these tips and you will find it easier to listen effectively. Truly effective listening leads to effective learning.

A Good Position

A key to listening well is to engage with the person who is speaking. Engaging with a person means focusing fully on what that person is saying and doing. You need to engage physically as well as mentally to listen well. Before a lesson begins, make sure you choose a good place to sit in your classroom. If you can see and hear the person talking, it is much easier to focus on them and concentrate.

Try to sit directly in front of the speaker.

These listeners are not engaged with the speaker.

CHOOSE YOUR POSITION

Remember that effective listening requires engagement with the speaker. Follow these tips to help you listen effectively:

- **Sit where you can clearly see and hear the speaker:** Sit away from windows and doors, where unwanted noise might reach you from outside the classroom.

- **If you can, face the speaker directly:** Try to sit with your front facing him or her.

- **Make yourself comfortable:** Be sure you are not too hot or too cold so you are not distracted.

REMOVING DISTRACTIONS

Another important tip for all kinds of listening is to make sure you are not distracted. Many things can distract you—friends talking around you, noises outside the classroom, people walking by. For effective listening, you need to be able to ignore distractions.

A Quiet Place

Most people find that their mind tends to wander from time to time. To help you focus only on what you are listening to, try to remove things that can distract you. Different things distract different people. Some people are distracted by other people talking. Others can't help looking out of the window, or thinking about what they will eat for dinner. Distractions such as these stop you from focusing on what a speaker is saying. To avoid distractions, try to create a peaceful and focused frame of mind—so you are ready to listen. It's a good idea to ask your fellow listeners to do the same. That way, you will all help each other.

These listeners are distracted.

Be Willing

You will also listen well if you decide you are ready and willing to listen and learn. Before you go to class, try to make a conscious decision to find out about the day's topic—and to find it interesting. You'll be amazed what a difference this positive attitude will make to your listening. It will put you in the right frame of mind to concentrate and gain knowledge.

STAY FOCUSED

Remember that effective listening requires quiet concentration. Try to follow these simple tips to be sure your listening is focused:

- Sit by quiet people who will not talk while you are trying to listen.
- Switch off your cell phone.
- Be committed. Effective listening takes effort.

It is easier to listen well in a quiet classroom.

LISTENING FOR DISCUSSION

Listening is particularly useful during a class discussion. You may be debating a topic in small groups, one-on-one, or the whole class might join in led by the teacher. In all these situations, you need to be able to listen to what other people are saying. If you listen to other people, you can then think about their opinions and respond with your own ideas.

An Open Mind

Effective listening in discussions begins with everyone having an open mind. This means being ready and willing to consider what other people have to say. Try to come to a debate ready to hear new information, ideas, and points of view. You will be more active in your listening if you try to avoid having fixed ideas about a topic. It's fine to have some knowledge and information of your own. However, do not assume that is the only knowledge there is. Keeping an open mind can be difficult, and it takes practice.

Always consider the opinions of others.

Come to class with an open mind, willing to learn something new.

No Agenda

If you come to a discussion with your mind already made up, you are more likely to have an agenda of your own for the discussion. This means you will be determined to put forward your own ideas and not consider others. This may be to convince others of your viewpoint, or to speak most often. However, having an agenda will not help you, or others, to learn.

KEEP YOUR MIND OPEN AND RECEPTIVE

TIPS FOR SUCCESS

In order to be able to listen to another person's point of view, you need to keep your mind open to new ideas. Before you listen to a debate, try to:

- Make a commitment to learn at least one new and interesting thing during every speech you hear.

- Remember that you are there only to listen to and understand the speaker. You do not have to agree with him or her.

- Listening with an open mind gets easier as you work at it. Practice, practice, practice!

BE ATTENTIVE IN DISCUSSION

It is much easier to concentrate on what someone is saying if you are looking at him or her. Learn to use your eyes as well as your ears when you are listening. It will make you a much better listener.

Maintain Eye Contact

If you slouch in your chair and look at the floor while someone is talking, you may easily get distracted. Try to be attentive in your body language. Sit up straight and look directly at the person speaking to you. Wherever you focus your eyes, your brain will follow. Continue to look at the speaker until they have finished talking.

It's easier to listen well if you sit upright in your chair.

Try to remain undistracted and focused on the speaker.

Look for Signs

Speakers may also give you clues to help with your listening. Listen for changes in the pace of their speech. They may slow down when they want to emphasize an important point. They may also repeat key information points. Look for the way they move around or use their hands for emphasis. Look out, too, for how they use their notes. They may use them more when communicating details or examples. That's a cue for you to listen particularly carefully.

EYES AND EARS

TIPS FOR SUCCESS

Try to use your senses of sight and hearing when you listen to a person speak. This will help you notice any clues the speaker gives as he or she talks. Here are some key listening tips to follow to make sure you look and listen well:

- **Keep eye contact with the speaker:** This direct line of contact will help you to concentrate.

- **Listen for variations in speech:** Look for changes in the pace and volume of the speaker's speech.

- **Fine-tune your listening:** Look for clues in the speaker's behavior.

BE PREPARED FOR DISCUSSION

When you are having a class or group discussion, you will find that you listen more effectively if you are well prepared. If you have some prior knowledge and understanding of a topic, it will be easier to take in what your teachers or classmates are saying, and then consider their opinions.

Advance Work

Before you come to class, read and study any materials you have been given beforehand. Find out as much as you can about the topic. Research the different opinions about your topic. Understanding that there is more than one point of view will help you be an active listener—knowing as much as possible about the topic will help you evaluate what you hear.

Research your topic before you come to class.

A library is a good place to research information.

A Step Ahead

Active listeners productively use the information they learn before a talk or discussion. If you have researched your topic, you will find it easier to concentrate as you listen to the speaker. You will not have to waste time trying to grasp the topic. This means you will have more time to take in new information and think about what is being said. If you are part of a group in a discussion, try to share with the other members of your group what you have learned so far.

TIPS FOR SUCCESS

BE PREPARED

Good preparation is key to improving your listening skills. It is always worth putting in time and effort before any talk or discussion to fully research the topic. Try to:

- Read advance materials you have been given.
- Extend your knowledge through background reading and research.
- Discover the different points of view related to your topic to further expand your knowledge.

MAKING CONNECTIONS IN DISCUSSION

In order to listen well, it is essential to concentrate and focus. Your brain works a lot better if you focus your thoughts on what a person is saying! When you concentrate, you hear new things and your brain starts making connections with what you already know. Focus for effective listening!

Speedy Brains

You can listen to and understand language around two or three times faster than a person can speak. That means you have a lot of spare capacity in your brain to think about lots of other things while you are listening. The downside to this ability is that you can get easily distracted if you are not focused on a speaker! A good listener knows how to use the spare capacity in his or her brain to think about what the speaker is saying.

As you listen, try to make connections with what you already know.

Focus your attention on the speaker.

Think It Through

If you are listening to a classmate in a discussion, try to think about how his or her viewpoint would work in practice. Follow the details of the argument, and test it out. Use what you already know to help you test the viewpoint. Ask yourself the following questions: Is the argument clear? Does it agree with what you already know or think? If not, could you be mistaken? How can you explore the topic further in your debate? By questioning the speaker's viewpoint as you listen to him or her, you will remain focused on what he or she is saying.

THINK, THINK, AND THINK AGAIN!

TIPS FOR SUCCESS

Now that you know your mind can become easily distracted, you can keep it in check! Remember that active listeners make connections. Try to follow these steps to make sure you stay focused on the discussion and listen to every word the speaker says:

- **Make connections:** Link what you are hearing to what you already know.
- **Think about the speaker's point:** Examine and test it.
- **Do you agree?:** Ask yourself whether or not you agree with the point, and how you can move the discussion forward.

CHAPTER FOUR

LETTING THE SPEAKER FINISH

You are concentrating on listening to the speaker. In your head you are making connections. You may then find you have lots of questions that you want to ask—and are impatient to know the answers. You may want to raise your hand to get the speaker's attention and ask your questions. Hold back, though—it's important to keep quiet and let the speaker finish.

Wait for the End

It is a courtesy to let a speaker finish his or her talk. They have something to say, and you should stay quiet while they are talking. Your mind may be racing, but try to just listen. You might miss something important if you speak up too soon. Often speakers make a useful summary at the end of their speech, or they save the most important material until the end. They will have thought about how to structure their speech—and often keep the best until last!

Keep your thoughts about the speaker to yourself!

Don't Interrupt!

It is tempting to jump in when you are really engaged with the topic, but try not to interrupt. Don't finish the speaker's sentences for them, and don't call out, "I knew that!" or "But...". Don't even speak up to agree with the speaker. Just listen! Your role is not to show how smart you are, but to listen and understand. Your turn to speak will come.

You may react strongly to the speaker, but stay quiet until they have finished.

JUST LISTEN

TIPS FOR SUCCESS

Remember that effective listeners stay quiet until the speaker has finished. Work on remaining patient and calm throughout a talk, saving your questions until the very end when you know that the speaker has finished talking. Try to keep these courtesy points in mind as you listen:

- Don't interrupt, even to agree with the speaker.
- If the speaker is arguing against your opinion, let him or her make the point. You will know the whole argument and be able to respond better at the end of the talk.
- Your role is simply to listen—that way you will be able to understand what the speaker is saying.

REVIEWING THE SPEAKER'S IDEAS

You have waited and listened patiently to what the speaker has to say. The speaker has finished his or her talk, and is now open to any questions you might have to ask. Now is the time to think about your response to the speaker's thoughts, ideas, and opinions in readiness for questions.

Yes or No?

Do you agree or disagree with the speaker? This is the point to bring together everything you have learned before the talk along with everything you have heard the speaker say. Using your previous knowledge and having listened attentively, you can now make up your mind about the speaker's presentation. Consider your response before speaking. Did the speaker add new information or insight that changed your view? Is your mind honestly open to being changed?

Remember to consider your response before you speak.

THINK FIRST

Remember that effective listeners think before they respond. Before you jump in with questions and opinions, take some time to work through your thoughts:

- Keep an open mind while you review the speaker's ideas. Try to curb your immediate reactions.
- Consider the ideas together with all the evidence provided by the speaker.
- Relate the speaker's evidence and ideas to what you learned before the talk.
- Respond when you are invited to, calmly and with authority.

Keep On Topic

It's a good idea to stop yourself from speaking up immediately after a talk has finished. Wait a little while before you jump in. It's tempting to speak first and speak loudest, but your first reaction may not be the best one. You will make a better contribution to the discussion if you think first, and talk later. Your response will then be on-target and will elaborate on what has already been said.

Take time to think carefully about questions before you ask them.

ASKING QUESTIONS

Another key to being a good listener is to ask great questions. During a group discussion, think carefully about what the speakers are saying. When a speaker has finished, ask well-informed questions to clarify his or her points or develop them further.

Listen to Understand

The point of listening is to understand. You need to check your understanding by asking yourself questions. This may not always be easy, but don't just give up and stop listening when the information is difficult. When the subject is hard to understand, you need to listen even more carefully. Do not be afraid to ask questions—it's a sign of intelligent listening. The key is to ask the right questions, and to also ask them well.

Asking great questions shows that you have been listening.

A speaker will be happy to explain any words you do not understand.

Clarify Meaning

If there are words you do not understand, make a note to ask about their meaning. Others in class will almost certainly not have understood the words either. It helps to clarify the speaker's argument if you ask questions such as, "So is it correct that you are saying ...?" If the speaker's point is not clear to you, you could ask, "Can you give me an example of ...?" Be sure to ask questions, rather than just stating your own opinion.

TIPS FOR SUCCESS

HOW TO ASK QUESTIONS

Asking questions after a talk is one of the most effective listening tools you can use. If you have listened well to everything the speaker had to say, you will be prepared to ask relevant questions. Before you direct your questions to the speaker, try to remember these points:

- First paraphrase the point the speaker made, to ensure you have understood him or her correctly.
- Ask questions about details of vocabulary or meaning.
- Don't be afraid to ask questions—everyone will gain value from them.
- Try to keep your questions relevant and do not go off the topic.
- Do not try to impress or influence the speaker. The aim of your questions should be to clarify the speaker's meaning.

23

CLARIFYING MEANING

Another important listening exercise is to summarize an informational text that is read aloud to you. Almost all of the tips already discussed in this book will help with this. There are some differences, however, from listening to speakers as part of a discussion.

Active Listening

As with all listening activities, to improve your comprehension you need to engage with the speaker, decide to concentrate, and make connections with what you hear. However, your task is to understand and summarize, not to respond. Your own reaction to the text is not important here. You are not required to evaluate and ask questions about a point of view presented by the speaker.

Summarizing a text
you have heard read
aloud is a great skill.

Check the Words, See the Words

If you are listening to an informational text, check that you understand the vocabulary. If you are not sure of the meaning of a word, think about the context in which it is being used. This will help you to understand the word. If you are still not sure, ask what the word means at the end of the reading, or look up the meaning in a dictionary. With a fictional text, it can also help to visualize what you hear, to make pictures of it in your head.

> Informational texts are part of everyday life.

LISTENING TO SUMMARIZE

TIPS FOR SUCCESS

Remember that effective listeners are actively involved. Here are some useful tips to help you summarize an informational text read aloud.

- Be comfortable, quiet, engaged, and willing to concentrate.
- Think about what you know about the topic and make connections.
- Find out the meaning of any words you do not understand.

TAKING NOTES

There is one tip that will help with all your listening in class, whether you are actively involved in a discussion or listening to a text in order to summarize it. If you can learn to do this one skill well, you'll find all your learning easier throughout school and college. That skill is to take notes.

In Discussion

When listening to a speaker in a discussion, you need to identify each point they make. You also need to know how they support each point with evidence. If you can take short notes about points and evidence while the speaker is talking, this will show you the structure of his or her argument. It will also highlight any gaps in the presentation, or in your understanding.

Use any clues the speaker gives you about the importance of the point they are making.

Taking notes helps keep you focused on being an active listener.

In Summarizing

Taking notes is also a key skill when listening to a text. Remember to follow the text carefully and take notes. However, you cannot write faster than the speaker can speak! Taking notes requires you to carefully choose what to write, which requires active listening. Remember, you are processing what you hear and deciding what is important.

HOW TO LISTEN WELL

You spend a large part of your school day listening. You listen to your teachers and to your friends. Sometimes you listen to find out instructions, sometimes to learn, and sometimes to get to know other people better. In all these situations, there is a lot you can do to make yourself a better listener.

Listen at Home

Practice good listening in your everyday life, too. It's a life skill that will help you in many ways. At home, listen to family members. Practice this when you sit at the table during meals. When you are with your friends, try to let one person speak at a time. Try listening to an informational program, such as the news or current affairs, on the radio instead of the television. It will help focus your listening.

Listening to each other makes us feel valued.

Practice Makes Perfect

Like any skill, good listening takes practice. Everyone finds that their mind wanders sometimes. With practice, you will learn when this is most likely to happen to you. You'll then be able to check yourself, and get your active listening back on track.

Good listening will help with every aspect of your education.

MAKE A CHART

A chart can be a useful tool that will remind you of the steps involved in active listening. Include the following points on your chart:

- Be prepared.
- Engage with the speaker.
- Remove distractions.
- Decide to concentrate.
- Make connections with what you know.
- Let the speaker finish talking.
- Ask questions.

Becoming a Great Listener

After a while, you won't need to use tools such as charts while listening. With lots of listening practice, you will start to listen effectively automatically. You will then be able to listen closely and gain knowledge and understanding, and be a great listener!

GLOSSARY

active listener a person who is concentrating and thinking about what is being said

assume to accept that something is the case without any proof or evidence

attentively with concentration

authority expert knowledge and confidence

capacity the amount that something can hold or someone can do

committed having made a decision to concentrate and learn

communication the exchange of information or opinions with another person

concentration giving your full attention or effort to something

connections links between one thing and another

context the background to the way something is said, that helps to explain it

convince to persuade someone that something is true or correct

debating exchanging opinions

distracted having your attention drawn away from something

effectively with a good result, well

elaborate to explain in more detail

emphasize to give special importance to something

evaluate to think about the value or worth of something

evidence facts or objects used to support the truth of something

extend to take further

informational text text that is not fictional, that is about facts

influence the power to affect another person or an event

insight being able to understand the truth about something

pace speed

paraphrase to use different words to show the meaning of a text

passive something that we do without thinking

perform to do something in front of other people

processing thinking carefully about

related relevant to

review to think about

structure how something is arranged

FOR MORE INFORMATION

BOOKS

Burstein, John. *Have You Heard? Active Listening*. New York, NY: Crabtree Publishing Company, 2010.

Buzan, Tony. *Mind Maps for Kids: Max Your Memory and Concentration*. London, UK: Thorsons Publishers, 2007.

Chin, Beverly. *How To Study For Success*. San Francisco, CA: Jossey-Bass, 2004.

WEBSITES

Discover more tools and techniques for listening and other study skills at:
kidshealth.org/kid/homework/classwork/studying.html

Find out how to stay focused in the classroom at:
www.wikihow.com/Pay-Attention-in-Class

Find out more about active listening and how to improve your listening skills at:
www.studygs.net/listening.htm

INDEX